GW00671784

THE EMPIRE AT WAR

JOHN BOWIE

B.T. Batsford Ltd, London

ISBN 0 7134 5777 5

Typeset by Latimer Trend Co. Ltd, Plymouth
and printed in Great Britain by
The Anchor Press, Tiptree
for the publishers
B.T. Batsford Ltd
4 Fitzhardinge Street
London W1H 0AH

INTRODUCTION

The Second Sikh War, 1848–49 *(figs 1–3)*

The earliest military photographs in India were taken by an officer in the Bengal establishment of the East India Company's army – surgeon John McCosh – who in 1848 and 1849 photographed some of the participants in the Second Sikh War. He was stationed at Almora in the foothills of the Himalayas and attached to the 31st Bengal Native Infantry Regiment. The Second Sikh War began with the murder of two British citizens: Mr Vans Agnew of the Bengal civil service and Lieutenant Anderson of the Bombay Fusiliers. Entering the city of Multan, they were attacked by Sikhs and killed; their severed heads were laid at the feet of the Diwan Mulraj of Multan, the self-appointed leader of the insurrection. In the resulting war John McCosh was present at many of the famous battles, such as Gujerat and Chilianwala.

The Second Burma War, 1852–53 *(figs 4–6)*

The Second Burma War was the next to produce any photographic images. Again John McCosh was present, now attached to the 5th Bengal Artillery. This campaign was in response to ill-treatment of British merchants by the Burmese, combined with the British desire to expand further east. A force was sent to attack Rangoon, and McCosh was able to photograph the city, pagodas and captured guns. He recorded the British defeat of the city of Prome, taking pictures of the troops, palaces and equipment; he used the calotype method, producing 10 by 8 inch pictures, as he had done in the Sikh War. This method used paper negatives, giving cheaply-made and coarse-grained pictures, not of the best quality but of great historical interest.

The Kaffir War, 1852

In 1852 war broke out in South Africa between the Cape colonists and the Kaffirs, the name given to the collective tribes of southern Africa. These tribes were being steadily driven back from the better farmland by the increasing number of colonists. The British faced difficulties as the tribes were well-armed with guns and the countryside was scrub and rock, making it easy for ambush and hit-and-run tactics to be employed by the natives. No photographs were taken of this war, the last campaign before the Crimean.

The Crimean War, 1854–56 *(figs 7–21)*

In Europe peace had reigned for the British since their victory at the Battle of Waterloo in 1815, but in 1854 Britain was once more at war with a European power, Russia. This time France was our ally, which caused problems for many of the senior British officers who had fought in the Napoleonic campaigns and, on more than one occasion, still referred to the French as the enemy, much to the embarrassment of the staff officers.

The war was caused by the Russians wanting to expand in the Balkans at the expense of the Turkish Empire, which was in decline; there was some pretence at protecting Christians in holy places, but this was purely cosmetic. This expansion was not in the interests of the British and French, who did not want a Russian presence in the Mediterranean, and Britain was particularly sensitive about her routes to India.

The War Department were worried by the adverse reports sent back by William Russell – *The Times* newspaper correspondent – and in June 1854 they decided to order a photographic expedition to the Crimea in order to provide the War Office with visual proof to establish or discredit Russell's accusations. As there were no military photographers the War Department appointed Captain John Hackett of the 77th Regiment to take charge and contract a civilian photographer. He approached Dickinson & Company, a Bond Street studio, who sent an employee, Richard Nicklin. The contract was for six months, to be extended as required, and the rate of pay was six shillings per day, plus rations. Corporal John Pendered and Lance Corporal John Hammond, both of the Royal Sappers and Miners, were selected to act as assistants to Nicklin; they were to receive two shillings per day. After a few days' instruction they set off for the Crimea taking with them 16 cases of photographic equipment, one large camera and one small camera, a dark tent, eight bottles of collodion and numerous other chemicals. As soon as they arrived they were hard at work. Several weeks later, with their photographs safely stowed, they boarded the supply ship, *Rip Van Winkle*, for the voyage home. In a freak storm outside the harbour of Sevastopol the ship foundered, taking with it the photographers and their unique pictorial record.

Undaunted, Captain Hackett applied for a replacement of equipment and photographers. This time they were military men, two young officers, Ensigns Brandon and Dawson. They were sent out in the spring of 1855, having received a month's training from one of the leading photographers of the time, J. E. Mayall. They produced a large number of images which were safely brought home, but which were of such inferior quality that they began to fade almost immediately. By 1869 they were in such a poor state that the War Office decided to destroy them.

William Russell's reports in *The Times* told of worsening conditions:

In the tents of our men the water is sometimes a foot deep, they have neither warm or waterproof clothing, they are out sometimes for 12 hours in the trenches in rain and snow. Beggars in the streets of London lead a life of princes compared with the British soldiers who are fighting for their country.

A political storm broke and the government fell. It was at this time that Roger Fenton, a photographer friend of the royal family, left for the Crimea. He was under the patronage of Queen Victoria and Prince Albert, and he had the assistance of the Secretary of State for War, the Duke of Newcastle. Thomas Agnew and Sons, the Manchester publishers, financed his expedition. As the images were to be sold to the public, he was told to avoid the ravages of war so as not to offend good taste!

He arrived on 8th March 1855 with his two assistants, William the handyman and cook, and Corporal Marcus Sparling of the 4th Light Dragoons, who drove the waggon and looked after the horses. He had five cameras and 700 glass plates, of which he used 360. The conditions were terrible, just as William Russell had reported. Complete chaos reigned in the British camp, and there was an extraordinary lack of co-ordination – a feature of the whole campaign. It is a tribute to the tenacity of the British soldiers that they won the war!

On his return to England Fenton was summoned by his patrons, Queen Victoria and Prince Albert, to show his pictures. Still weak from cholera, contracted at the front, he was allowed to lie on a couch while he talked to them. Her Majesty was shocked and dismayed by what she saw. Later she commanded that the returning wounded soldiers were to be photographed at Chatham when she visited her troops. There she was confronted by the sad sight of many wounded and limbless soldiers.

Fenton's work in the Crimea was

continued by James Robertson, who arrived when the final battles were under way. Robertson, like those before him, was restricted in the amount of action he could record. His images of the destruction of the Mamelon and Malakoff fortresses recall the First World War, such is the devastation and ruin. Like Fenton's, Robertson's images were for sale. He also sent some to *The Illustrated London News*, who used them as a basis for their engravings in the magazine. Again, like Fenton, he photographed no corpses or mutilated remains.

On the Russian side Count Tolstoi, who was with the army at Sevastopol for eight months, took photographs which were displayed in Moscow. A Romanian photographer, Carol Popp de Szathmari, photographed scenes of both sides, Turkish and Russian, and was permitted access into the battle lines. Neither side seemed to be troubled by this potential breach of security, although his photographic waggon attracted artillery fire. Roger Fenton was also attacked when his waggon came within the range of the Russian guns at Sevastopol.

The war ended in April 1856, with the signing of a peace treaty in Paris.

The Indian Mutiny, 1857 *(figs 22–31)*

The year following the Crimean War saw the British in conflict in India. The mutiny of the East India Company's army began on 15th May 1857, and quickly spread to Delhi, the old Mogul capital of India. There were several causes of the Mutiny: non-payment of the local troops who had fought in the Punjab, missionaries trying to convert the soldiers to Christianity, and even the loss of the free posting of letters. The grievance most remembered, however, was the issue of new cartridges for the Enfield rifle. The cartridge had a paper covering that had to be bitten open before it was inserted into the barrel of the rifle. This paper was greased and it was

the common belief that it was smeared with beef and pig fat, forbidden to Hindus and Moslems respectively.

The main areas of revolt were the central provinces and the recently annexed kingdom of Oudh. Most other parts of British India remained calm. The recapture of the city of Delhi, the spiritual capital of India and the heart of the rebellion, was the chief objective of the army. It was besieged on the second week of June 1857, and assaulted on 14th September. The advance through the city was slow and painful; the fighting was street-by-street and house-by-house until, on the sixth day of fighting, the last rebel strongpoint fell and the Union Jack flew over the city again.

Meanwhile, at the city of Cawnpore, General Sir Hugh Wheeler was under siege at the barracks, which contained 900 people, half of them women and children. They held out for three weeks and then, on the promise of safe conduct, they left the garrison for boats on the River Ganges. The mutineers, however, had no intention of keeping their promise, and the entire British contingent was shot, hacked to pieces or drowned. The relief British force arrived soon after and the pitiful sight of this ruthless murder of men, women and children made every soldier determined to exact a fearful revenge for this atrocity.

No prisoners were taken, no quarter given or asked. Mutineers who fell into British hands were hanged or given a 'Cawnpore dinner', six inches of cold steel. Photographs depict the shattered buildings and the infamous prison where the Europeans were held.

At Lucknow there were 1,700 British and loyal Indian troops who took refuge in the residency and held out under siege against some 60,000 rebels. A relief force reached them under General Havelock in September 1857 at a cost of 500 casualties. They were too few to raise the siege and it was not until the 17th November that Sir Colin Campbell fought his way to the city and defeated the

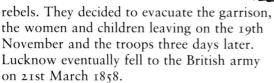

rebels. They decided to evacuate the garrison, the women and children leaving on the 19th November and the troops three days later. Lucknow eventually fell to the British army on 21st March 1858.

Photographs were taken of the ruins by Felice Beato, who was in partnership with James Robertson, having been with him in the Crimea. This time, dead bodies were photographed as was the hanging of rebels.

The revolt continued until early February 1859, but, by this time, had become a mopping-up operation and more of a guerrilla war. The Mutiny brought an end to the rule of the East India Company, who had managed British India as a private company. Its army was incorporated into the British forces. In 1876, Queen Victoria was proclaimed Empress of India, and the country was regularly garrisoned by British regiments.

China, 1860 *(figs 32–35)*

After two years of peace the British were at war again, this time with China and again were allied to the French. In 1860, broken treaties and the reluctance of China to open their country to trade, plus the need to defend the profitable opium trade through Hong Kong, caused the British to send a force to the East. On August 21st 1860, General Sir Hope Grant – of Indian Mutiny fame – led a 17,000 strong British and French army and stormed the fortresses at the head of the Hai river. The forts were taken and the way opened to the city of Tientsin. Felice Beato photographed the forts and the dead Chinese soldiers. The Allies occupied Tientsin and waited for the Chinese government to ratify the treaty. Meanwhile the Allies advanced on Peking. A party of interpreters and 26 soldiers were sent under a flag of truce to the Chinese.

Talks were held with the intention of making the Allies complacent. A series of incidents made the truce party realize the

danger, and some escaped back to the Allied army; unfortunately others were captured. The Chinese committed themselves to battle with an army of 30,000 men; the British and French numbered a mere 3,000. After a two hour engagement, the Chinese were utterly routed. Two more actions were fought on the road to Peking, and a Chinese general was mortally wounded. Once more, letters passed between the Chinese and the Allies demanding terms and the return of the prisoners who had been under the flag of truce. The Allied army had increased to 10,000 strong, and Peking was entered without bloodshed. The Emperor's Summer Palace was systematically looted. It was here that the fate of the prisoners was discovered: tied by their feet and hands with wetted cords, which had shrunk and become tighter, in order to cause more pain, they had been left in the sun to die, kicked and abused in a barbaric manner by the Manchu soldiers. As the Summer Palace was the scene of these atrocities the Allies ordered it to be levelled with the ground. Millions of pounds worth of loot was carried off by the Allies, and out of it a sum was set aside for the murdered prisoners' relatives. Peace was negotiated and settled by the end of the year.

Ambela Expedition, North-West Frontier, India, 1863 *(figs 36–39)*

Hindustani fanatics had caused trouble on the North-West Frontier since 1860; they had also harboured Mutineers from the East India Company. These fanatics had raided over the River Indus and had built up a subversive organization with Bengal Moslems. In 1863 a campaign was launched to destroy their power, an army of 5,000 men was dispatched to skirt behind the Hindustanis and drive them forward towards the waiting second army. This required the army to pass through the country of the Bunerwals north of Ambela. To preserve secrecy of the plan as long as possible the Bunerwals were not informed of the British plan. The fanatics took the opportunity of telling the Bunerwalis people that the British had come to destroy them, and that they should join the Hindustanis in crushing the British army.

The small army found itself confronted by some 25,000 tribesmen. The general decided that the best course of action was to defend the pass and wear down the enemy. Pickets were posted on each side of the valley, where the mountains rose to 5,000 feet to protect the army below. Day and night skirmishes broke out between tribesmen, short and bitter actions often hand-to-hand. British re-enforcements arrived at the end of the year and as the Bunerwals had suffered heavy losses they were ready to come to terms. They offered to destroy the Hindustanis stronghold at Malka, which they did in concert with the British. They also promised to keep them out of their country. The three-week campaign became a three-month war, and nearly a thousand men were killed or wounded.

New Zealand, 1861–1866 *(figs 40–44)*

The war in New Zealand lasted, on and off, for over ten years. It was caused by the greed of the colonists who began to take excessive quantities of land from the Maoris. The first campaign lasted from 1861 to 1862. The British troops only numbered about one thousand men and were heavily outnumbered by the Maoris, who were brave and clever fighters. The Maoris would build a fortress called a pa. After a bombardment by the artillery the British would advance, only to find that the Maoris had slipped out of the back into the dense forests.

The fighting died down until the British started to build a road straight towards Maori lands in 1863, and war broke out again. The Maoris made a stand at Orakau where 300 of them held off two thousand well-armed

British soldiers. After a three-day bombardment the Maoris again charged out of the pa and in the confusion half of them disappeared into the swamps and forests to fight another day.

In 1864 the Maori king's village was captured, but the war was continued under a 'no-surrender' policy. Most of the British troops left New Zealand in 1866, leaving the colonists to carry on the fight. Sporadic fighting continued until 1872, but some of the Maori tribes never gave in to the government.

Abyssinia, 1867 *(figs 45–50)*

The Emperor Theodore of Abyssinia received Sir Charles Cameron, a British diplomat in 1862. Sir Charles had brought gifts from Queen Victoria. The Emperor was well pleased and wrote to the Queen advising her that he intended to send a diplomatic mission to London. Unfortunately his letters were overlooked by the Foreign Office. As the months passed the Emperor became paranoid and thought that there was some conspiracy against him. In 1864 he detained Cameron and his staff, together with all the other Europeans in Magdala, the fortress capital. By the time negotiations had proceeded between London and the Emperor it was 1866; he seized the negotiators and put them in prison. The British realized that force would have to be used to release the prisoners, and an army was gathered under the command of General Sir Charles Napier. He was determined not to repeat the fiasco of The Crimean War, and his preparations for the advance on Magdala were very precise. Troops 12,000 strong assembled at Zula on the Red Sea coast, with 20,000 baggage animals, half a million pounds sterling in gold coins – the only currency accepted in the country –4,000 Snider Enfield rifles, three hospital ships, and a team of photographers from the 10th Company of the Royal

Engineers. This was the first time that photographers were officially taken on a campaign. They carried two cameras, together with the plates and lenses on mules.

First contact with the emperors army was at the Arogié Pass. The new Snider Enfield rifles in the hands of the disciplined British troops devastated the enemy, combined with a bayonet charge that left 2,000 dead and wounded Abyssinians on the field.

At Magdala, heavy artillery fire and a direct assault by the British soon resulted in the fall of the citadel. The Emperor shot himself in the final moments with a revolver that had been sent as a gift by Queen Victoria! The British prisoners were released, together with Abyssinian prisoners who had been incarcerated for up to 30 years by the Emperor Theodore. After destroying the fortress and carrying off the Imperial Crown of Abyssinia, the British retired back to the Red Sea coast. The campaign was a complete success with the loss of only 35 British troops.

The Ashanti War, 1873

The Ashanti War of 1873 was fought on the west coast of Africa in the sweltering heat of the dense jungle. The Ashanti – a fierce and war-like people, feared by their neighbouring tribes, fought the British for the sixth time in 70 years. Many years before they had murdered a British diplomat and used his skull as a drinking cup. They had extended their harsh slave-based rule over much of the area later known as the Gold Coast Colony. At this time British rule was mainly confined to the coastal strip.

General Sir Garnet Wolseley was put in command of a special task force to crush the military power of the Ashanti. It had to be achieved inside two months before the March rains made the fever-ridden jungle inaccessible. Arriving on the 1st January 1874, the army, heavily dosed with quinine,

marched north. At Amoafu – 20 miles south of the capital Kumasi, the 2,200 man force found the Ashanti army on the 31st January. The battle was soon over; the reckless bravery of the Ashanti warriors was no match for breech-loading rifles and the steady discipline of the British soldiers. Hundreds of Ashanti were killed, including three of their noblest chiefs; the rest turned and fled into the jungle.

The army advanced on Kumasi and entered the capital on the 5th February 1874. The capital stank of blood and appalled British soldiers found the remains of several thousand human sacrifice victims, executed in an attempt to appease the gods and stop General Wolseley's advance. Having set light to the city, burnt grain and muskets and removed gunpowder, the army returned to the coast. The Ashanti agreed to pay an indemnity of 50,000 ounces of gold and keep the peace. No photographs were taken on this campaign and Ashanti was not annexed by the British Empire until 1902, and then only because of the fear of French or German interference.

The Afghan War, 1878–1880 *(figs 51–59)*

In 1878 the increasingly friendly relations between the Afghan Amir Shere Ali and the Russian Czar Alexander II led to a second war between Great Britain and Afghanistan. Though never part of the British Empire, Afghanistan was always a sensitive border state for both Britain and Russia. A British force invaded the country at three points; 12,000 men under General Stewart moved towards Khandahar, 6,000 men under General Roberts entered the Kurram Valley and 15,000 men under General Browne moved into the Khyber Pass. The columns under Stewart and Browne were not confronted, but on the 2nd December 1878 General Roberts met an Afghan army of 18,000 men at Piewar Kotal. The British general skilfully turned the

Afghan position and routed them, causing heavy casualties and capturing all their artillery.

Peace was concluded in May 1879 and the Amir accepted a British mission headed by Sir Louis Cavagnari. In less than four months, however, Cavagnari had been murdered. After a very gallant defence of the mission against overwhelming odds, the Indian soldiers who died in the process were all posthumously awarded the Indian Order of Merit, the highest decoration for the Indian army. General Sir Frederick Roberts marched into Afghanistan once more and occupied the capital, Kabul. He found the new Amir, Yakub Khan, nephew of Shere Ali, was too weak a character to control the Afghans. In the south of the country the Amir's younger brother Ayub Khan, a stronger personality, had decided to drive the British out of Afghanistan completely. A British force of 2,500 men was sent out to meet the Afghans at Maiwand, 50 miles north of Khandahar. The British were outnumbered ten to one; the result was a catastrophe for the British, The British artillery shot off all its ammunition in an attempt to snatch a quick victory, leaving the British and Indian troops to be overwhelmed by sheer numbers; a third of them were killed. Those who escaped were besieged in Khandahar.

General Roberts promptly marched south, covering the 313 miles in 22 days which was surprisingly fast considering there were freezing temperatures in the early morning rising to 110°F by noon. The skin peeled from the faces and the hands of the soldiers. They rose at 4.00 am and after an hour's march rested ten minutes; breakfast was at 8.00 am; at noon, camp was set up for the night. Dust storms caused delays and rations had to be cut.

On 1st September 1880, General Roberts brought the Afghans to battle by outflanking them with a feinting movement. The deception worked perfectly, and the whole of

the Afghan artillery was captured. After desperate fighting with fixed bayonets, the British inflicted 2,000 casualties on the Afghans, destroying their army. General Roberts returned a hero, and was later raised to the peerage with the title 'Lord Roberts of Khandahar'. Several photographs were taken during this campaign by James Burke who had made a record of archaeological surveys in the north-west provinces of India in the late 1860s. After the Afghan War, Burke specialized in army photographs until 1907.

The Zulu War, 1879 *(fig 60–63)*

After the British occupied the Transvaal in 1877, there was continual friction between the British and the Zulus. The British government did not want to have a powerful native state on its borders which was not only independent but had a tradition of warfare as a way of life. A British army crossed the border on the 22nd January 1879 consisting of 7,000 regular troops and 7,000 Natal Province levies. At a place called Isandhlwana, as the army bivouaced, the main Zulu army of over 30,000 warriors attacked them. The British suffered a loss of 1,600 men. When the relief column arrived later, photographs were taken showing the shattered waggons and the unburied bodies of the soldiers who fell in the struggle.

General Lord Chelmsford pressed on towards the Zulu capital at Ulundi; at Gingindlovu the British army was attacked on the 2nd April 1879 by a large Zulu force. This time there was no element of surprise, and the Infantry opened fire at 400 yards with breech-loading rifles and Gatling machine guns. After 20 minutes the Zulu army crumbled, leaving a thousand dead on the field. No warrior came nearer than 30 yards to the British square.

Two more actions were fought at Hlobane and Kambula before the final push to Ulundi. The Zulu king's capital was guarded by

20,000 warriors and on the 4th July 1879 the final battle of the war was fought. The British were in square formation by 8.00 am that morning, awaiting the attack. The Zulus rose out of the tall grass, regiment after regiment, springing to their feet to form a vast horse-shoe shape. The British fixed bayonets to their guns and formed four ranks – the front two kneeling. At 9.00 am the guns opened fire at a range of 2,000 yards, and as the Zulus advanced, the artillery changed to case-shot. Nine-pounders drove bloody lanes through the warriors. The dead lay in heaps, and again no Zulu came within 30 yards of the square. As the Zulus faltered, Lord Chelmsford ordered the cavalry out of the square and commanded them to charge the now-fleeing enemy. In half an hour it was all over. Over one thousand Zulus were killed. The British lost 15 men, and 78 were wounded. Later, the Zulu king, Cetywasho, was captured and the war came to an end.

Numerous photographs were taken on this campaign, including individual portraits, camp scenes, battle fields and group pictures. The camera was beginning to be part of the war scene. Wood-cuts were made from the photographs and used to illustrate magazines and papers before actual photographic printing methods were established.

The First Boer War, 1881 *(fig 64)*

When the Boers in the Transvaal revolted to establish their own republic, they besieged the small British garrisons in the area. On the 28th January 1881 General Sir George Colley marched inland from Natal with an army of one thousand men. At the pass of Laing's Nek, the Boers blocked the way. The British attacked the strong position and were repulsed, with a loss of almost 200 men in the process; Boer casualties were only 14 dead and 27 wounded. The British then regrouped and moved forward to occupy Majuba Hill which commanded a vital pass through the

mountains. Taking advantage of faulty deployment by the British, the Boers made a dawn attack on the 27th February 1881. The British were swept off the hill, losing 280 men out of a total of 550; General Sir George Colley was among the killed. This battle resulted in independence for Boers and the formation of the South African Republic.

The Egyptian War, 1882 *(figs 65–67)*

In 1880 an Egyptian army colonel, Arabi Pasha led a revolt against the government. The causes were many and in retrospect legitimate; pay was poor or non-existent, the higher ranks were controlled by Turkish officers instead of Egyptian, and conscripted soldiers were used for cheap labour on menial tasks. The revolt had some success, and by 1882 Arabi Pasha became minister of War. Worried about the control of the Suez Canal and the safety of the European population in Egypt, the British sent warships to Alexandria and demanded the dismissal of Arabi Pasha. He began to build fortresses at Alexandria, which the British ordered to be dismantled. After the British had sent an ultimatum to the Egyptian government, Law and order began to break down. There were riots and looting of shops, and some Europeans were killed. On 11th August the Royal Navy bombarded the fortresses, reducing them to rubble. The Egyptian army withdrew from Alexandria, leaving the city to the mob. A British landing party then occupied the city and restored order.

General Sir Garnet Wolseley marched inland with 17,000 men. On 28th August 1882, after the British had captured the water supply at Kassassin Lock, they were heavily attacked by the Egyptian army at 4.30 pm. Ammunition supplies were getting low, owing to the thick sand bogging down the reserve ammunition waggons. An aide was sent to get support from cavalry division, who were some four miles away. By the time the cavalry reached Kassassin it was nearly dark; a thick haze covered the desert, but a bright moon was shining. As they came under rifle fire, the Cavalry rode straight at the guns and the Egyptian Infantry. In seconds they were amongst them; the heavy cavalry swords rose and fell, cutting and slashing at the unfortunate infantrymen. The Egyptians were cut to pieces, their Artillery withdrew, followed by their Cavalry, leaving the decimated Infantry to withdraw as best it could. At 8.15 pm the British were back in camp with only 27 killed or wounded.

At Tel-el-Kebir the Egyptian army stood some 22,000 strong. They had constructed a line of earthworks and redoubts running for about four miles into the desert. The whole line was fronted by a ditch with sloping sides, 6 feet deep by 9 feet wide. They also had 9- and 14-pounder German Krupp guns dug into the defences. To the front was hard sand completely open and without cover. Consequently General Wolseley decided on a night attack; at 1.30 am the 17,000 strong British army moved forward at a steady pace. After one and a half hours march they halted and rested. At 4.55 am the Egyptians sighted the Highland Regiments 200 yards in front and opened fire. The Highlanders fixed bayonets and advanced with pipes playing. Initially the Egyptian army fought well, particularly the Sudanese battalions, but the position was finally carried by the British after about three quarters of an hour's fighting. By 5.30 am, the battle was over.

At 7.00 am General Sir Garnet Wolseley was greeted by his cheering men as he rode through the ranks. The operation had been a complete success with only 57 killed and 412 wounded on the British side. The Egyptian forces had a death toll of over 2,000 and many more were wounded. Meanwhile, the British cavalry galloped the 50 miles into Cairo and received the surrender of the garrison. That night Arabi Pasha and his chief officers also surrendered their swords.

They were court-martialled by the Egyptians and the death sentence passed was commuted to exile for all of them.

The Sudan War, 1884 *(figs 68–72)*

In 1884, the British sent General Gordon into the Sudan to supervise the evacuation of the people from a religious fanatic known as the Mahdi, or 'The Expected One'. Gordon arrived in Khartoum and evacuated 2,500 Egyptian men, women and children. He asked for aid from the British army but the politicians hesitated. For ten months General Gordon directed a spirited defence by the Egyptians, but on 26th January 1885, the Mahdist forces stormed the city in overwhelming numbers and put everyone to the sword, including General Gordon.

The relief expedition under General Sir Garnet Wolseley, having fought its way up the Nile and over the desert, arrived two days later only to find the Mahdis black flag flying over the city. The army withdrew into Egypt, fighting a rearguard action all the way. At Suakin – a port on the Red Sea – the Egyptian and British forces had been fighting a supporter of the Mahdi, Osman Digna, a slave trader of some influence in the area. After the fall of Khartoum, reinforcements were sent to protect the construction of a railway at Suakin where the port was virtually under siege. Osman Digna had been defeated in battle but only after a fierce and costly contest.

The reinforcements comprised 13,000 men, including the Royal Engineers who photographed the campaign, as they had done in the Abyssinian War. The company consisted of one N.C.O. and six men. They had a waggon fitted up as a darkroom and carried two cameras, and six lenses, one wide angle, and one rapid rectilinear for copying maps.

The army made a reconnaissance in force and came in contact with the enemy at

Hashin. There followed an indecisive engagement with the Mahdist force, and the British withdrew to Suakin. Having decided to establish outposts to protect water and supplies, a large force set out from Suakin, marching in squares for protection. Because of thick scrub and difficulty of maintaining formation after six hours of gruelling marching, it was decided to set up a camp at Tofrek. As they were building the Zariba – an enclosure of thorn bushes used as protection against attack – the Mahdist host rose out of the scrub in their thousands and threw themselves at the British. As one man, they sprinted for their stacked rifles inside the zariba. The Berkshire Regiment formed rallying squares as the Dervishes swarmed around them, overrunning the Gardner machine-guns and spearing their crews. The battle was fought in thick clouds of dust and sand as well as smoke from the gun-fire. There was savage hand-to-hand fighting between spear and bayonet, but eventually the steady discipline of the British soldiers backed up by the fire power of the breech-loading Martini-Henry rifles, broke the impetus of the Dervishes and they fell back.

As the battle was progressing, the colonel of the regiment, who was surveying the scene from his charger, was suddenly attacked by four Dervishes. The Colonel calmly drew his revolver and shot each one dead through the head, with complete accuracy. He then returned to watch his men repulse the hordes of Dervishes. After the action the regiment was granted the prefix Royal by Queen Victoria; the only occasion when such an honour was awarded for a single action. It was a costly battle with about 300 dead and wounded on the British side; the Dervishes lost over 2,000 dead and wounded; those injured had little chance of recovery. The British soldiers were surprised to see the Dervish casualties with shaven heads, but it transpired that Osman Digna had had a vision a few days before in which the prophet had told him that shaven heads would make his men bullet-proof. It was clear from the heaped up corpses that something must have gone drastically wrong!

In the weeks that followed the Dervishes lost heart and peace was in the offing. Word came from London that a complete withdrawal from the Sudan had been decided upon because of a Russian threat on the Indian North-West Frontier – a far more serious prospect.

Burma, 1885 *(figs 73–75)*

In the first two wars with Burma, in 1824 and 1852, the British annexed only part of the kingdom, leaving the greater part in the hands of the native ruler. In 1885 a more serious threat developed when King Thibaw virtually invited the French – who had developed considerable influence in Indo-China – to establish a protectorate over his country and oust the British. When the king threatened British traders the Viceroy of India had the excuse he needed to invade the country. On 14th November 1885, an army of 9,000 men advanced up the Irrawaddy River by steamer; when they reached the royal capital at Ava, King Thibaw surrendered. Mandalay fell on 28th November, and the war was over. King Thibaw died in exile during the First World War in Bombay.

Burma had been formally annexed to the British Empire on 1st January 1886, as a New Year's present to Queen Victoria! The Burmese army had, however, disappeared into the dense jungle to carry on a guerrilla war, roaming the country as Dacoits or bandits, preventing orderly administration from being carried out. Eventually 32,000 troops were required to placate the country, and it was not until 1891 that the campaign ended, although as late as 1900 there were 20,000 armed police in Burma.

India, 1891, and Chitral, 1895 *(figs 78–80)*

There was a rising in 1891 on the North-West Frontier of India three years after some previous unrest. The Black Mountain tribe actively resisted a column of British troops marching in the Black Mountain area. An expedition was dispatched in the spring of 1891 to restore order and an uneasy peace settled on the Frontier for a while until Chitral, 1895.

When the Khan of Chitral was murdered in 1895 by a usurping member of his own family, the British Resident in Chitral accepted the situation as best he could under the circumstances. In April of 1895, an escort of Indian soldiers was attacked, and in the following skirmish the British officer and about 40 of his men were killed. Fourteen of the soldiers fought their way back to the British fort and held out until captured by an act of treachery; 68 boxes of ammunition were also captured by the Khan's men. The British Resident was besieged for 46 days in his fort and one fifth of the garrison were killed. Many incidents of bravery occurred during that time, as soldiers fought with swords and bayonets against desperate odds. On one occasion, the enemy ran a mine up to the walls of the fort, but the attack was thwarted when an officer and 100 of his men charged out, and bayoneted 35 of the enemy Chitralis – in the process, the British blew up the gunpowder, sending a further 60 of their number up in the blast. A blast which sent their souls to heaven and their charred pieces of remains back to earth, as one eye witness put it. The British relief column eventually fought its way through, and the Khan of Chitral surrendered, having lost too many men and villages to continue. At his surrender he wore a Russian officer's greatcoat with the military buttons of the Czar's army. His coat, like his politics, was reversible!

Tirah, North-West Frontier, India, 1897 *(figs 76–84)*

The North-West Frontier of India was once more the scene of conflict in 1897, this time in the state of Tirah. A large force of British and Indian regiments marched into the country, which could only muster about 50,000 fighting men. At Dargai, a small village with commanding heights, a battle was fought against 12,000 tribesmen. The British and Gurkha Regiments were pinned down by a withering fire until the Gordon Highlanders, with extraordinary bravery, took the heights at the point of the bayonet. The pipes played as they surged forward. The Regiment lost 36 men and 159 were wounded. A Victoria Cross was awarded to Piper Findlater, who, although shot in both ankles, continued playing the pipes under fire until the battle was won. The army followed the retreating tribesmen and there ensued a series of small but gallant actions. Eventually the war was over and the tribesmen submitted to an uneasy peace.

The Atbara, The Sudan, 1898 *(figs 86–87)*

The Sudan had been left to the mercy of the followers of the Mahdi until 1898 when Her Majesty's Government decided once more to attempt the re-conquest of the country. It was in 1896 that the Sirdar of the Egyptian army, General Kitchener, had methodically pressed up the Nile until he reached Berber, building a railway as he moved on. In January 1898 British troops arrived and were placed under the command of the Sirdar. One brigade was sent on up the Nile to where it divides in two, here they built a fort. One of the Khalifa's commanders, the Emir Mahmud, was sent with an army to crush the invaders. As the British advanced up the Atbara tributary of the Nile, the Dervish host crossed the desert to reach them and at the river they built a zariba (a palisaded enclosure) and dug rifle pits. On 7th April the British army advanced to within 900 yards of the enemy, here they rested and watered, awaiting the dawn.

At 6.20 am the British Artillery opened fire with shell and shrapnel; they also fired rockets which started fires. Machine-guns kept the Dervish Cavalry at bay, and after one hour and twenty minutes the barrage was lifted and the Infantry advanced over the desert. At 250 yards they fired in volleys, which were replied to for the first time by the Dervishes: men began to fall. The zariba was quickly pulled aside and the fight for the trenches and rifle pits began. The soldiers fought their way through, shooting and bayoneting. Most of the Dervishes held their ground until they were killed. At 8.25 am the bugles sounded 'cease-fire' and the battle was won. The British/Egyptian army losses numbered 80 dead and 479 wounded while 2000 Dervishes lay dead. The Emir Mahmud was captured and taken back to Berber where the army rested in summer quarters before advancing on Omdurman.

Omdurman, 1898 (figs 88–92)

The British army was considerably reinforced at Berber and on 24th August the final advance was begun against the Khalifa with 8,200 British troops, and 17,600 Egyptian and Sudanese. At the end of the month General Kitchener arrived at Omdurman, opposite Khartoum, on the banks of the Nile. After he had shelled the city, the Khalifa decided to give battle to the British outside in the desert. His force numbered about 50,000 of mixed Cavalry and Infantry. At 6.00 am on 6th September the British Cavalry scouts brought the news that the enemy was advancing rapidly. As soon as they came within the range of the Artillery they opened fire; this was about 2,700 yards. The Grenadier Guards and the Warwickshire Regiment opened fire first with their Lee Metford bolt-action rifles

that held a magazine of ten bullets. The Maxim machine-guns were brought into action and the whole British front was swept by such a fire that nothing could survive; the field was heaped with a quivering mass of the dead and dying. Few of the Dervishes got within 800 yards.

At 8.00 am the line advanced in extended order. Seeing a group of Dervishes rallying, the 21st Lancers formed line and charged the group. As they advanced they realized that the undulating desert had concealed a much larger number of Dervishes than they had anticipated. The 21st Lancers were outnumbered by 400 to 3,000. Never hesitating, they charged through the enemy at full gallop, a mass of hacking, screaming and slashing men. On the other side they re-grouped having lost 70 men and 119 horses. The colonel then dismounted his men and they fired volley after volley into the Dervish mass, who eventually broke under the galling fire and retired.

As the British advanced towards Omdurman they were attacked by the reserve force of the Khalifa, some 17,000 strong. At 1,200 yards the lethal firepower of disciplined troops overwhelmed the fanatical courage of the Dervishes and they broke off from the battle; by 11.00 am it was all over. About 10,000 Dervishes lay dead on the battlefield and thousands were wounded with little hope of recovery. The cost to the British was 48 dead and 434 wounded. The 21st Lancers having suffered the worst casualties.

General Kitchener entered Khartoum in the afternoon. The Khalifa escaped out of the rear of his palace as the troops battered down the front gates. He was killed the following year, with his loyal lieutenants, in a battle with a British force. Osman Digna was captured, and General Gordon's death was finally avenged.

The Second Boer War, South Africa, 1899
(figs 93–105)

The long-standing hostility between the British and the Boers hardened with the discovery of gold. The Orange Free State allied itself to the Transvaal on 11th October 1899, and war was declared the next day. The British suffered several reverses in one week. Firstly at Stromberg where, misled by guides, the troops blundered into a murderous fire before they could withdraw; 89 were killed and 600 were taken prisoner. At Modder River the Boers had built a heavily-manned position situated in a river bed, invisible to the British army. By persistent assault the British forced the Boers to retire, but at a cost of 24 officers and 460 men. At Magersfontein the British made a frontal attack against an entrenched position. The Highland Brigade were shot to pieces at 400 yards and suffered 700 casualties, including their brigade commander, who was killed. The British withdrew after suffering further casualties. At Colenso, despite the gallantry of the British frontal assault, the Boers held their ground and returned a deadly fire. The Royal Artillery were left without support and nearly all the gunners were killed. General Sir Redvers Buller, having suffered more than a thousand casualties amongst his troops, decided to call off the attack.

At this point General Lord Roberts was put in command of the British forces in South Africa. General Buller, however was to suffer another disaster at Spion Kop where there were nearly 2,000 casualties. When the Boers counter-attacked the Kop, senior British officers became casualties and the junior officers were uncertain as to their orders. General Buller admitted defeat and retreated back across the Tugela River. But gradually, in spite of all this incompetence, the British forces gained control of the situation, and at Paardeberg, with Lord Roberts in command, the Boers were defeated and surrendered.

General Buller – on his fourth attempt – relieved Ladysmith and the war ended when Lord Roberts entered Bloemfontein in May 1900. There followed a guerrilla war until 30th May 1902, when hostilities finally came to an end.

China, 1900 (The Boxer Rebellion) *(figs 106–110)*

The steady annexation of Chinese territory by Europeans in the latter part of the nineteenth century, led to widespread anti-foreign feeling in north China. The Empress Tsz Hsi encouraged the 'secret society of harmonious fists' – the so-called Boxers – to attack the Europeans. On the outbreak of violence, the British admiral, Sir Edward Seymour, led an international expedition to Tientsin, where they were fired upon from the Taku forts by the Chinese. In Peking the Boxers promptly rose and killed the German minister Baron Von Ketteler. They then laid siege to the foreign legations on 20th June 1900. A six-nation expeditionary force landed on 14th July at Tientsin, and marched the 80 miles north west to Peking, fighting all the way. At Peking the legations suffered their heaviest attack from the Boxers, but it was too late; the European troops were already entering the city. The Empress fled, as did all the Chinese soldiers and Boxers. Altogether 66 people were killed in the foreign legations and 150 were wounded; peace, retribution and an indemnity ended the war, and the Empress returned to the Imperial Palace.

Tibet, 1903 *(figs 111, 112)*

Fear of Russian influence in Tibet caused the government to send a military mission to the capital, Lhasa. Colonel Francis Younghusband led 3,000 men across the border and, after fighting three actions, halted at Gyangtse in April 1904 to organize supply lines back into India. The army waited here until June, expecting the Dalai Lama to negotiate a settlement. As this was not forthcoming, the army advanced on to the capital Lhasa. An action was fought and the city was entered. Later a treaty was signed and the British withdrew into India. The Russians were busy elsewhere, fighting the Japanese – recent allies of the British.

Zakha Khel Expedition, 1908 *(fig 113)*

A punitive expedition of 14,000 men was dispatched against the Zakha Khels on the North-West Frontier of India in 1908 under Major General Sir George Wilcocks. The tribesmen had been raiding across the border and their audacity culminated in a raid on Peshawar itself. With the employment of the new ten-pounder mountain gun, and well-trained troops this campaign was over within three weeks.

Some small wars and actions have not been included in this collection because of the lack of photographs or because they were not interesting enough. Hundreds of actions were fought in Africa or the North-West Frontier of India; many were not photographed at all but as the nineteenth century progressed it is surprising how many officers began to find room in their kit for a box Brownie camera. The majority of these images are of groups or views, but occasionally there are photographs of great historical interest, they may lack the professional touch and composition but 'they were there'. If some pictures appear not up to the standard we expect, remember the circumstances in which the image may have been taken.

1. General Sir Charles Napier, Commander-in-Chief of India, 1848

Famous for his conquest of the Sind country of western India in 1843–4, which became part of the Indian Empire. His military strategy in this campaign was warmly praised by the Duke of Wellington. He became Commander-in-Chief of India in 1849, but resigned the following year after a disagreement with Lord Dalhousie. The general died in 1853.

2. *Major Daniel Bamfield, 56th Native Infantry, 1848*

Major Bamfield was one of the 89 officers who were killed and wounded at the Battle of Chilianwala in the Second Sikh War on 13th January 1849. His regiment lost 8 officers and 322 men within minutes under a shower of grapeshot and musketry from the Sikhs. The Major died later from the wounds he received in the battle. This conflict against the Sikh army was particularly hard-fought and resulted in a stalemate. Even so, the Sikh forces withdrew from the field. The British suffered casualties totalling 2,357 men from all ranks.

3. *Captain Robert N Tronson, 2nd Bengal European Regiment, 1848*

This regiment also fought in the Second Sikh War and were present at the battle of Chilianwala, and in the following battle of Gujrat. Here the British laid down a two-hour artillery barrage before advancing upon the Sikh position. The regiment lost a total of 149 from all ranks in the following engagement. The regiment were made into Fusiliers for their services in the war. They later became the 'Second Battalion of the Royal Munster Fusiliers', before disbandment in 1922.

4. Soldiers outside a Burmese pagoda, 1852

*Four regiments were detailed for service in this campaign: 18th
Royal Irish Regiment, 35th Royal Sussex, 51st Light Infantry
and the 80th Staffordshire Regiment. They are wearing their
undress caps with white covers as protection against the sun.
The sweltering heat accounted for more British deaths than did
bullet wounds.*

5. *British officers with artillery, Burma, 1852*

*The officer on the right is wearing a pith helmet, soon to be
very familiar in India. This early model was made of wicker
instead of pith and had a crested ridge top. In the background
are captured Burmese artillery pieces.*

6. Indian soldiers at Prome, Burma, 1852

Prome was taken in October of 1852 and resulted in the annexation of Lower Burma to the British. These soldiers are sepoys of the East India Company's army from Madras and Bengal. A total of 4,388 soldiers took part (the Burmese army mustered 50,000 at this time). British artillery was used with deadly effect on the massed Burmese: the round shot made lanes through the ranks causing gruesome injuries.

7. The recruit, 1856

This photograph by Roger Fenton – taken at the time of the Crimean War – depicts a country fellow who appears to have accepted the Queen's shilling and joined the army. On the right stands a recruiting sergeant from the Infantry, and on the left one from the Cavalry. The demand for recruits at the time of the Crimean War was high and a bounty of ten pounds was paid; by the mid-1860s; this had been reduced to one pound. The kit and the uniform was free, and the pay was one shilling per day; three pence extra was paid in the Cavalry. During the Crimean War there was a field allowance of six pence per day for every man. Length of service was twelve years in the Cavalry or ten years in the Infantry.

8. *The Grenadier Guards at Haider Pasha, June 1854*

This is one of the earliest photographs of the Crimean War and depicts the Grenadier Guards in Turkey. They are wearing the white linen trousers worn in summer; several are wearing their bearskin caps. The battalion was camped here from June until September, carrying out extensive field training with unsuitable equipment and in very hot weather. They landed in the Crimea on 14th September and a few days later fought the Battle of Alma.

9. Cornet John Wilkin, 11th Prince Alberts own Hussars, 1855

*As assistant surgeon, Wilkin rode with the 11th Hussars in the
Charge of the Light Brigade and subsequently purchased a
Commission in the Rank of Cornet. He was an excellent
horseman and organized races in the spring of 1855. He is
depicted in all the finery of this crack regiment, which is the
full dress uniform, less the embroidered saddle cloth.*

10. Survivors of the 'Charge of the Light Brigade', 1855

*These men are from the 13th Light Dragoons who were on the
right of the line. Lieutenant Colonel Doherty stands fifth from
the left. Cornet Denzil Chamberlayne seated on the ground in
the centre had his horse shot from under him but he was
unhurt and walked back to the British lines with his saddle; he
remarked, 'another horse you can get, but you will not buy
another saddle so easily'. A total of 362 horses were killed in
the charge and 260 officers and men were killed or wounded.*

11. A quiet day at the battery, Royal Artillery, 1855

_This is a siege mortar; 35 of these 13 inch land service mortars
were used in the Crimea. Much of the fighting in this war
consisted of bombardments and counter-bombardments
between the Russian and Allied artillery. There was also the
occasional sortie by the Russians. The British gunners were
armed with muskets and bayonets and the officers usually
carried revolvers._

12. *Camp of the 97th Earl of Ulster's Regiment, Crimean War, 1855*

The regiment arrived in the Crimea on 20th November 1854; they were immediately sent forward to join the light division in the trenches before Sevastopol. The Russians made a raid in strength on the trenches early in the following year and although outnumbered ten to one, the regiment repulsed them, inflicting severe losses. At the attack on the Redan Fortress they met the full brunt of the Russian fire: Out of 360 officers and men, 212 became casualties.

13. *Two Cavalry sergeants, Crimean War, 1855*

*Both men are wearing the gold-laced forage cap and the blue
stable jacket. The sergeant on the left has the regulation dark
blue overalls with a red stripe, his companion is wearing non-
regulation thigh boots, popular with the Cavalry during the
war. It is difficult to determine from which Cavalry regiment
they come, except that the sergeant on the left has the crown
and harp above his stripes denoting the 8th King's Royal Irish
Hussars. The other might be from the 4th Light Dragoons.*

14. *A meeting of the Commanders-in-Chief, 7th June 1855*

Seated on the left is the British commander, Lord Raglan, who had fought his last battle at Waterloo, where he lost his arm. In the centre sits the Turkish general, Omar Pasha, a Croatian Moslem convert who had defeated the Russians in Silestria in 1854. On the right sits the commander of the French army, Marshal Jean-Jacques Pelissier, who took command in May 1855. A British officer described him as 'a very fat, coarse, vulgar looking man, more like an old coalminer than a general, however, he is one of the right sort.'

15. Quartermaster John Hill, 4th Light Dragoons, 1856

John Hill was present at the Charge of The Light Brigade. The horse he is sitting on was the one he rode then and a survivor of the hard winter. His boots are non-regulation and his pistol holsters at the front of the saddle appear to be empty. This officer was also a veteran of the Afghan War of 1838–40.

16. *Cavalry camp at Balaklava, 1856*

From early in 1855 prefabricated wooden huts (as seen in the background) were sent out from England to replace the inadequate tents. The horses suffered from the winter weather as well a the battles and many died. During the spring and summer of 1855 the officers organized races, shooting and fox hunting.

17. Officers in the 4th Queen's Own Light Dragoons, 1856

*These gentlemen are in a relaxed mood smoking their cigars;
the seated officer on the left is wearing a French officer's kepi.
On the right stands an officer in a civilian waistcoat and a hat
which is definitely not regimental. They are standing outside
the wooden huts that were transported from England for the
use of officers, owing to the poor accommodation available for
the soldiers in the second winter, the huts were made available
to all ranks.*

18. Balaklava Harbour, 1856

This was the main supply point for the British army in the Crimea. Less than 300 yards wide it was permanently crowded with all types of shipping. In the early months of the war conditions were chaotic and the organization ramshackle, but gradually matters improved. Prince Albert sent out 20 gamepies and 20 cases of soup to every battalion, as well as two tons of tobacco. The Duke of Wellington, colonel of the Rifle Brigade sent 30 dozen bottles of brandy out to the troops.

19. *Lieutenant General Sir Henry William Barnard, Grenadier
Guards with his Staff, 1856*

The General commanded the 3rd Division on his arrival in the
Crimea and became Chief-of-Staff six months later. A brave
and popular officer, he also had the distinction of being the
owner of the horse that was Napoleon's Marengo's grandson.
The young officer seated with the general is from a Dragoon or
Dragoon Guard regiment. The two officers on the left are from
Infantry regiments.

20. *Allied camp on the plateau before Sevastopol, 1856*

*In high summer the temperature often exceeded 100°F and the
tents were adequate. However, as the winter months set in
conditions became appalling. Corporal Fisher of the rifle
brigade wrote, 'so many are crowded in one tent, when your
comrades come in wet, tired and covered in mud you get a
good share of wet and mud from them if you are not in the
same state yourself. If you sit down it must be in the doubled-
up position, if you lie down you get kicked and trodden on by
all comers.*

21. The Reverend Henry Wright, principal chaplain to the army with other chaplains, 1856

There were only seven chaplains in the whole of the British army in 1855. Reluctantly the War Department increased their numbers to 22 at the end of the war, and they were given commissions in the army. The chaplains devoted much of their time to the wounded at Scutari in Constantinople, where drunkenness among the convalescent soldiers was rife.

22. *Ferozepore Artillery, Punjab, 1856*

*At the outbreak of the mutiny the Punjab was relatively calm.
All important posts were secured, suspect native regiments
disarmed, and mutinous leaders executed. In spite of this, the
British officers placed their pistols beside their plates at dinner
and on the pews at church. Mutineers were tied to the muzzles
of guns such as these and blown to pieces as the artillery fired.*

23. *Bengal Horse Artillery, 1857*

This elite and elegant regiment was the pride of the Bengal army at the outbreak of the Indian Mutiny. All the officers and troopers were European. The short jacket and riding overalls were of dark blue, heavily-laced in gold or yellow braid. The collar and cuffs were red. The helmet in the Roman style had a leopard-skin turban, and a scarlet-horsehair plume fell from the crest. The dark blue saddle-cloth was embroidered with the regimental crest and battle honours. It was also edged in gold or yellow lace. At the end of the Indian Mutiny when the East India Company's forces came under the power of the Queen, the three brigades were reconstituted as the 2nd and 5th brigades of Royal Artillery.

24. Part of the barracks held by General Wheeler, Cawnpore, 1857

Cawnpore was an important city on the road between Delhi and Benares. The Europeans were under siege in the barracks from 6th until 27th of June 1857. Incessant fire by day and night from the 24-pounder guns dashed the defences to pieces. The dead were heaped up and thrown down a well, under the cover of darkness, by the defenders. Babies were shot in their mothers' arms. Lieutenant Wheeler – the General's son – was killed sitting on a sofa with his sister when a round shot crashed through the wall and decapitated him. The soldiers are from the relief force, the 1st Madras Fusiliers.

25. *The Bibighar, or 'House of the Ladies', Cawnpore, 1857*

General Wheeler surrendered his force of 150 men and 300 women to the Indian Mutineers and accepted the use of boats to get them away. Reaching the river, a bugle sounded and concealed Infantry opened fire. The mutineers rode into the river and sabred many. The 206 women and children who survived were placed in the Bibighar. On the approach of the British in July, soldiers were sent to kill the women and children but they had no stomach for it, so two butchers were sent in with knives. Next morning the women and children were dragged out – some still alive – and were thrown down a well. When it was full of bodies the rest were thrown in the River Ganges.

26. The hanging of Mutineers, Indian Mutiny, 1858

*Each day the gallows had the fresh fruits of rebellion displayed
upon them, so wrote the Deputy Judge Advocate, General F.
Thurburn. The news of the massacre at Cawnpore and
elsewhere had prompted wide-scale hangings when anyone
suspected of being a Mutineer was caught. Brigadier General
Henry Havelock said, 'there must be no more disbandments
for Mutiny. Mutineers must be attacked and annihilated and if
there are a few in any regiment who are not immediately
announced to be shot or hanged, the whole regiment must be
deemed guilty and given up to prompt military execution.'*

27. The Kashmir Gateway, The Red Fort, Delhi, 1858

The city of Delhi was the focal point of the Mutiny, and its recapture was imperative. The British besieged the city from June 1857 until September of the same year. Four columns of men attacked the fortress (8,000 men in all), and a party of engineers was sent to try and blow up the Kashmir Gate. An officer ran across the shattered bridge and placed a bag of gunpowder against the gate, then dropped down into the ditch in a hail of bullets. The sergeant who followed was killed, but the next sergeant managed to place two bags of powder for an officer to light the fuse. The officer was shot dead as well as another sergeant before this could be done. Just then a fuse in one of the bags exploded, shooting the masonry and timber from the gate into the air. The British soldiers poured through the shattered entrance in a hail of fire, yelling and cursing, hacking with their swords and bayonets at the defenders, trampling over the dead and dying.

28. *The residency at Lucknow, 1857*

*This large and imposing government building was constructed
in 1780. It looked down on the huge city of 600,000 people and
was placed under siege by the Mutineers from July 1857. Sir
Henry Lawrence – the resident – was killed by a shell which
burst through the wall, completely shattering the lower part of
his body. Below ground in the cellars, and in any spot that
offered protection from shot and shell, some 500 women and
children suffered the rigours of the siege. This photograph –
taken in the following year – depicts the terrible devastation
caused by the Artillery.*

29. *The gate of the small Imam Barra, Lucknow, 1857*

*On 25th September a relief force reached Lucknow, but was
not strong enough to raise the siege. On 17th November
General Sir Colin Campbell raised the siege and was able to
fight his way out with the garrison. The city was then occupied
by the Mutineers. It was not until March the following year
that Lucknow was recaptured by the British. This photograph
was taken then, with a group of 1st Madras Fusiliers at ease.*

30. *British soldiers on the roof of the Alumbagh, 1858.*

*This house was the favourite residence of the King of Oude's
senior wife, and was three miles from the city of Lucknow.
The casually dressed British soldiers are waiting for the final
advance on the city which was made in March of that year by
Sir Colin Campbell. These men are dressed in the various
costumes adopted during this hard fought campaign, with a
number of different weapons thrust through their belts. A
ladder against the tower wall leads up to an observation point
to view the city of Lucknow.*

31. The Secondra Bagh, Lucknow, 1858

On the final assault of the Mutineers' defences two 18-pounder cannon breached the walls. When enough had been broken to permit three or four men to enter the 93rd Highlanders forced their way in together with the 53rd Regiment and the 4th Punjabis. Memories of Cawnpore unleashed retributive rage amongst the Highlanders; in the 120 square yards nearly 2,000 Mutineers fell; the ground was covered with dead and writhing bodies. Upstairs they fought from room to room; the Highlanders killed them all, hurling the bodies – dead and alive – from the windows to the ground below.

32. *The Pehtang Fort at the mouth of the Pehtang River, China, 1860*

This photograph shows the sprawling fortress at the start of the China War of 1860. This was the third war with the British, brought about by failure to ratify the Treaty of Shanghai and demands for indemnities and apologies for past treatment. The British were allied to the French in this war and acted in concert with them. The Chinese were found to have concentrated their main forces at the Taku forts, about ten miles south at the mouth of the Pei Ho River. In the photograph, the Allies had taken possession and were encamped within the walls.

33. Inside the Pehtang Fort, China, 1860

The fort at Pehtang was found to be deserted when the Allies
arrived, the Chinese having decided that the Taku forts were
stronger. Inside the Pehtang Fort it was found that the Chinese
had left arms, cannon and many stores. Sitting in the shade are
some British soldiers.

34. *Outside the defences of the North Taku Fort, 1860*

*For more than three miles in front of the forts there extended a
field of slimy mud. Directly in front of the walls of the fort
was a continual line of pointed stakes. As the British advanced,
knee-deep in mud and holding scaling ladders above their
heads, they were met by a hail of cannon shot, arrows, and
pots filled with caustic lime.*

35. Dead Chinese on the ramparts of the North Taku Fort, 1860

On 21st August 1860, the Allies attacked the North Fort –
thought to be impregnable by the Chinese. The British
bombarded the fort from dawn and at 7.00 am the magazine
inside blew up. The Chinese gunners had kept up a furious
cannonaed throughout the action, in part because their officers
had tied them to their guns! The Chinese lost 2,000 in the
action; the British suffered 212 casualties. The magazine
explosion was described as 'a tall black pillar bursting like a
rocket after it had attained great height, and with a great
shower of wood, earth and human remains returned to earth.'

36. Major Alexander Carnegy and the 2nd Belooch Infantry,
_1860_

_The Indian officers stand on the left with the British officers in
the centre. The regiment had been raised in 1846 and was
known as an extra battalion to the 1st regiment. Their uniform
was dark green tunic with scarlet braid on the collar and cuffs,
their turbans were also green; the trousers were red. The
officers are wearing the undress pillbox cap in place of the pith
helmet, their usual headdress._

37. *View of the walls of the city of Peking, October, 1860*

This is the wall of the Tatar city that encloses the Imperial city wall. As the Allies advanced towards Peking they sent envoys under a flag of truce to negotiate an agreement with the Chinese government. These men were brutally murdered after suffering torture. Their bodies were discovered at the Summer Palace outside the city walls; the palace was systematically looted and burned. A British officer found a strange little dog which he rescued and presented to Queen Victoria; the dog, named Looty, was the first Pekinese to reach England.

38. *A picket on the lookout, Ambela Expedition, North-West Frontier, India, 1863*

A major campaign was launched in 1863 against Hindustani fanatics in the Black Mountain area of the North-West Frontier. Advancing through the Ambela Pass, the 5,000-man British force was attacked by the Bunerwals, who were thought to be neutral. To guard the camp in the pass below, piquets were posted on the pine-covered slopes. Fierce fighting ensued, attack and counter-attack was a night and day occurrence. A British officer observed that the Gurkhas, who followed the enemy some distance were ripping them open and beheading their victims with their sharp kukries. A three-week operation became a three-month campaign with a loss of 238 killed and 670 wounded. The tribes suffered 3,000 casualties. The power of the fanatics was broken.

39. *The Craig Picket, Ambela Expedition, India, 1863*

British officers and Indian soldiers outside their tents. On the extreme left stands a Gurkha, and soldiers from the 3rd Sikhs. This was one of the small pickets scattered over the mountain pass to protect the British camp below. The tribesmen would suddenly appear, and a short and bloody fight would ensue. This was typical of the type of warfare on the North-West Frontier.

40. British troops at Rangiowhia, February, 1864

In order to reduce the Maori forces who were occupying strategic fortresses called pas, it was decided to cut off their food supply from Rangiowhia. On 20th February 1864 an assault was made by the British which resulted in its capture. The fact that it was a Sunday and the place was occupied by women and children went against the Maoris' sense of fair play.

41. The Paterangi Pa, February, 1864

The day after the skirmish at Rangiowhia the pa was abandoned by the Maori warriors. They moved to the top of Hairini hill and were attacked by the British 50th, 65th, and 70th Regiments. With a great cheer they swept up the hill and stormed the defences, The Maoris broke and withdrew into the swamps.

42. *Maori prisoners held in the Rutland Stockade, Wanganui, 1865*

The British soldiers standing at the back are wearing the campaign dress adopted in New Zealand; a blue jacket with brass buttons and dark blue trousers with a red welt down the seam. The head-dress was the undress pork-pie cap with a brass regimental badge. The uniform was adopted not only because the red cloth had failed to arrive from England, but because the terrain was extremely rough, including high fern and scrubland, as well as swamps.

43. *A and C Company of the 18th Royal Irish Regiment on parade with their goat, Rutland Stockade, Wanganui, 1865*

The stockade was so called because it had been constructed by the 58th Rutlandshire Regiment; it can be seen in the background. The men are wearing the dark blue uniform issued for the campaign in New Zealand. This regiment had arrived in 1863 and were engaged in most of the Maori campaigns until 1870. They were the last British regiment to be withdrawn from New Zealand.

44. *The 57th West Middlesex Regiment on parade at Wanganui, 1865*

The men are wearing the full-dress scarlet uniform worn only for special parades during their stay in New Zealand; The officers on the left are wearing the undress uniform. The regiment arrived from India in 1860, and served in the first Taranaki War and fought at the battles of Katikara and Poutoko in the second Taranaki War. They remained in New Zealand until 1866, when they returned to England.

45. *Zula Camp, Abyssinian War, 1868*

Zula was the landing point of the British expeditionary force. The camp consisted of about 50 tents and marquees, piles of hay and grain bags, hundreds of baggage animals, cases of ammunition and arms for the army, 3,000 horses, 16,000 mules, 5,000 bullocks, 8,000 camels and 44 elephants. Engineers from the Indian army soon converted the village into a bustling port.

46. Officers at Senafe, Abyssinia, 1868

This photograph shows Major Brown and Captain Hills at
Senafe, which is 60 miles from the coast approachable only by
a difficult ravine. This made it five days' march from Zula.
Magdala – the ultimate goal – was 400 miles away through
unknown and hostile country, and then there was an equally
exhausting journey back.

47. 27th Bombay Native Infantry, Abyssinia, 1868

This regiment came to the war complete with 16 buglers and drummers. The British officers are drawn up at the front of the regiment. The dress of this Corps was very splendid – red turbans with dark green tunics, and scarlet breeches. The men are from Baluchistan, and the regimental title eventually was changed to the 27th Baluchistan Light Infantry. It was for services in the war that the regiment was honoured by the change of title to 'Light Infantry'.

48. *Addigrat Camp, Abyssinia, 1868*

The progress to Magdala was methodical; ten miles a day was the steady advance made. At each camp a store was set up and a small guard mounted to protect it, ready for the return march. The men are gathered around the cooking stove eating a meal. It was not until the army was nearly at Magdala that the Abyssinians gave battle at Arogié. The hail of British gunfire tore into the massed Abyssinians killing and wounding about 2,000; the survivors turned and fled.

49. *The Royal Naval Brigade at Goon Goona Rock, Abyssinia, 1868*

The Royal Navy had disembarked with the Army at Zula and also made up part of the expeditionary force into the interior. They were armed with rockets which can be seen in the front rank. They caused havoc amongst the advancing Abyssinians at the Battle of Arogié, one hissing rocket just missed the Emperor Theodore during the conflict.

50. Entrance to Magdala, Abyssinia, 1868

The Fortress of Magdala was perched on a mountain top and contained the Emperor Theodore and his army. The battle for the place began with an artillery bombardment at 2,700 yards. The British troops advanced up a path guarded by two gates, each four feet wide. The 33rd regiment found their way round and two men hoisted themselves over a wall. Shooting every Abyssinian who appeared, they rushed forward and secured the second gate and then fought their way back to the obstinate first gate. Magdala soon fell and the Emperor shot himself with a pearl-handled revolver; the war was over.

**51. Camp of the Peshawar Valley Field Force, Afghan War,
1878**

*This view looking towards the heights held by the Afghans at
Ali Musjid. The British army advance guard, under the
command of Brigadier General Appleyard, attacked the right
flank, the Royal Artillery opening a heavy and effective
covering fire. All day there was no abatement of the Afghan
fire and, as night fell, the British decided to hold their positions
until the following morning. During the night the Afghan army
retreated, leaving the heights in British hands.*

52. *Captured Guns on Shergai Heights, Afghan War, 1878*

*Here Brigadier General Appleyard and his staff stand with
captured Afghan artillery. After the British took this position,
it was ascertained that the enemy's strength was about 4,000
and the defences were almost impregnable; if they had been
attacked there would have been an immense loss of life. As it
was, the British suffered 49 casualties.*

53. Officers of the 51st regiment (King's Own Light Infantry), Afghan War, 1878

The regiment was engaged in the front attack at Ali Musjid, coming in range of the enemy's fire about 1.30 pm and going into action two hours later. Six companies occupied various advanced positions and remained engaged until dark. The casualties of the regiment during that day comprised one dead and two wounded. They remained at Ali Musjid until 19th December 1879 on the further advance of the main division.

54. *Group of field telegraphers, Afghan War, 1878*

*In India the Madras Corps of Sappers and Miners opened an
army school in 1874 to teach telegraphy. As well as the electric
telegraph, signalling was taught to regimental sections, and the
use of the heliograph for the close control of a battle was
found to be very effective. The Times report of the Battle of
Armed Khel was telephoned to a heliograph station and then
to the field telegraph head. It was then telegraphed to the
junction of the field telegraph and the extended civil system.
The report was published in London the next morning.*

55. *The attack on Peiwar Kotal, Afghan War, 2nd December 1878*

General Sir Frederick Roberts, with an army of 6,000 British troops, was attacked by an Afghan army off 18,000 men. The General skilfully turned the enemy position, capturing all their artillery and inflicting heavy casualties.

56. Mountain artillery ascending Spin Cawai Kotal, Afghan War, 2nd December 1878

As part of General Sir Frederick Roberts' plan, this kotal was captured, and the Artillery men were able to shell enemy positions on Peiwar Kotal. Under a galling fire and finding their line of retreat threatened, the Afghan army withdrew, leaving behind vast quantities of stores and ammunition besides all their artillery.

57. Field Hospital, Afghan War, 1879

*The Army Medical School, after many delays, was founded in
1860 at Fort Pitt, Chatham; it then moved to Netley near
Southampton, on accessible position for the incoming hospital
ships. After training officers were sent out to their regiments,
and gradually a fairly competent field medical service evolved.
The Indian army had its own army medical services along
similar lines to the British. Dramatic progress was made in
surgery in the last half of the nineteenth century, and the
soldiers' chances of recovery were much increased.*

58. *Sherpur outside Kabul, Afghan War, December 1879*

The peace of May 1879 ended with the murder of the British mission under Sir Louis Cavagnari. General Sir Frederick Roberts defeated the Afghans at Cherasai and entered the capital, Kabul. The small army had to winter at Sherpur outside the city in an entrenched position. On 23rd December they were attacked by 100,000 Afghans, who were defeated after six hours of fighting. British reinforcements then arrived, comprising 7,000 men, led by General Stewart.

59. *R*oyal Horse Artillery battery at rest, Afghan War, *1879*

Nine batteries of Royal Horse Artillery fought on all fronts
during this campaign. At the disastrous battle of Maiwand on
27th July 1880, an untrained Indian regiment fled, allowing the
Afghans to overrun the position. The 66th Berkshire Regiment
fought steadily back-to-back until they were all killed. In this
action the Royal Horse Artillery Gunners fired shrapnel, which
killed hundreds of Afghans. The guns were nearly overrun and
67 of the horses killed; fierce hand to hand fighting took place
as they limbered up and retired to 400 yards then opened fire
once again with case shot. Twenty two gunners were killed
and 16 wounded in this action. Sergeant Mullane and Gunner
Collis were awarded the Victoria Cross, and eight others were
awarded the Distinguished Conduct Medal.

60. Mounted Gatling field battery, Royal Artillery, Zulu War, 1879

This battery was the first of its kind in the British army and was formed by No 10 battery, 7th brigade. Behind the gun stands Major J. F. Owen. This weapon was used by the Royal Navy and the Royal Artillery and consisted of ten rifled barrels revolving around a central shaft, fed from a cylindrical magazine placed on top of the barrels. It was fired by rotating a handle; the whole thing was mounted on a gun carriage. It fired a .45 calibre round and had an effective range of 1,200 yards; the rate of fire was 400 bullets per minute. A devastating weapon in the hands of trained gunners, its drawback was that it tended to heat up quickly and in prolonged action was prone to jamming.

61. 91st Highlanders, 1st Battalion Argyll and Sutherland Highlanders, Zulu War, 1879

The regiment arrived as reinforcements after the disaster of Isandhlwana where nearly 2,000 men had been killed by the Zulus. The 91st Highlanders had marched to the relief of Eshowe, which was under siege. In the following battle the steady rifle fire of the British regiments was no match for the Zulus, despite their determined and spirited attack. They fell in hundreds under the Gatling and rifle fire. The regiment wear tartan trousers except the pipers who can be seen wearing the kilt.

62. 2nd Battalion, the Royal Scots Fusiliers, Zulu War, 1879

The regiment is at church parade, in the centre stands the padre and to the left, the commander of the regiment – Lieutenant Colonel Collingwood – who was with the battalion throughout its war service. At the Battle of Ulundi the regiment formed part of the right side of the British square and bore the brunt of the first Zulu onslaught.

63. Part of the British camp before the Battle of Ulundi, 4th July, 1879

The British fought in a square formation, being the best defence against undisciplined troops. At 8.00 am on the morning of 4th July the British square halted to await the Zulus; they soon appeared – some 20,000 strong – and began the attack. The soldiers fixed bayonets and formed four ranks, two of them kneeling. At a range of 2,000 yards the Artillery opened fire – changing to case-shot as the range shortened – ploughing bloody lanes through the Zulus. The Infantry fired in volleys under the direction of their officers. The effect of such devastating fire was a foregone conclusion despite desperate bravery, no Zulu came within 30 yards of the British square alive. When the Zulu attacks wavered the Cavalry left the square and followed the fleeing Zulus. In half an hour the battle was over with more than 1,000 Zulu warriors dead on the field.

64. 6th Inniskillin Dragoons at the Tugela River, South, Africa, 1881

This photograph shows the troopers watering their horses at the time of the First Boer War. This war was an unmitigated disaster for the British, who lost every battle with appalling casualties. With Gladstone in power, the government quickly gave in to the Boer demands, and the army was unable to retrieve its honour. A republic was established right in the middle of British South Africa.

65. *Sailors from the British fleet inspecting the devastated forts at Alexandria, Egypt, 1882*

The rise of Arabi Pasha and worries over the Suez Canal caused the British to send a fleet to Egypt. Having received no reply to the ultimatum, the eight battleships and eleven gunboats opened fire. By evening the Egyptian guns had been silenced and the Egyptian army retired into the interior of Egypt leaving the city for the mob to loot, burn, rape and pillage. It was not until the British landed on 14th July 1882 that order was restored.

66. Dead Egyptian gunners in the ruined fort, Alexandria, 1882

The fortresses along the sea at Alexandria extended for about four miles; they were mounted with 180 guns. On 10th July 1882, the British issued an ultimatum that unless the forts were surrendered within 24 hours they would be fired upon by the British fleet. No word was received and the bombardment began. The Egyptians served their guns well but were poorly led and directed; they did little damage to the British ships. Watching from the flagship was a young engineer officer, who had slipped ashore in disguise to spy out the defences the week before; his name was Lieutenant Horatio Herbert Kitchener.

67. *The battlefield of Tel-el-Kebir, 13th September 1882*

*Crushed pith helmets, skulls and parts of unburied bodies litter
the Egyptian trenches. It was across this hard, sandy gravel
that the British army advanced in the dead of night and total
darkness, guided only by the stars. At 4.55 am contact was
made with the Egyptians some 200 yards in front of their
trenches. Swept by rifle fire, the British charged forward
bayonets fixed. By 5.30 am all resistance had been overcome.
The dead Egyptians numbered 2,000 and many more were
wounded. British casualties numbered 469.*

68. *1st Battalion, The Queen's Own Cameron Highlanders, 1884*

In November 1884 the regiment joined General Wolseley's expeditionary force which was sent up the Nile to rescue General Gordon. The regiment had come no further than Korosko when news came that the Dervishes had captured Khartoum and murdered Gordon. When the British army withdrew back into Egypt the Camerons were the rearguard force who held the Dervish army back. On the last day of December 1885, together with reinforcements from Egypt, they fought the last battle of the campaign at Ginniss. The Dervishes were completely defeated with heavy losses and retired back into the Sudan.

69. *R*oyal Engineer non-commissioned officers, Suakin, 1885

Three companies of Royal Engineers including a balloon
section and two telegraph sections were sent to Suakin in the
Sudan. Lieutenant General Graham, with a force of 13,000
men, was sent to crush Osman Digna, one of the Mahdi's
followers at the battle of Tofrek, 22nd March 1885. A
telegraph line had been laid – roughly buried in the sand – by
the advancing British square. Corporal Bent, the operator, had
to break transmission from time to time, grab a rifle and help
repel the Arabs. This was the first time in a front line battle
that the telegraph had been used.

70. *The troop-ship Jumna at No. 3 pier, Suakin, 1885*

*This was one of five troop-ships built in 1866 for the
government of India, and painted in the colours that
distinguished troop-ships until the end of their day: white with
a red riband round the hull and a yellow funnel; the riband
colour varied from ship to ship. They were designed to carry a
full battalion of infantry with their married families, or about
1,200 people. Jumna was the most unpopular of the five, owing
to continual engine trouble. On 6th February 1884, the 10th
Royal Hussars embarked at Bombay for Suakin together with
the M Battery, 1st Royal Artillery and the 2nd Battalion, the
Royal Irish Fusiliers. They arrived at Suakin on the 18th
February, 1884.*

71. *The West Redoubt, Suakin, 1885*

To protect the port of Suakin and the supply line General
Graham established outposts to hold back the tribes. A high
tower on a sandbag base was constructed as a lookout post.
Two pieces of artillery faced out over the desert behind the
thorny zariba of cut mimosa. From the tower, the soldiers
could signal back to base by heliogrpah if attacked in force.

72. *Otao, a view towards the wells, camp at the front, 1885*

In 1885, a railway was being built from Suakin to Berber on the Nile, a distance of 200 miles away. This was to link up with the army who should by then have occupied Berber. By the end of April the railway had reached Otao, 20 miles from Suakin. At this point the government in England decided to withdraw completely from the Sudan, owing to Russian threats on the Indian frontier.

73. 2nd Battalion the Devonshire Regiment attacking a stockade, Burma, 1885

The remaining part of independent Burma was annexed to the British Empire after a short campaign in November 1885 for fear of French expansion in south-east Asia. The soldiers are armed with the Martini-Henri rifle of .45 calibre. Some 70 rounds of ammunition were carried by each soldier, with 30 extra rounds available in time of war.

74. Guns being dismantled at Ava by the Royal Artillery, Burma, 1885

Ava was the royal capital on the River Irrawaddy. When the British army captured the city, King Thibaw surrendered. A force of 9,000 men advanced up river by steamer, one of which can be seen in the background. With the fall of Mandalay the war was over.

75. Dacoits giving up arms, Burma, 1885

The Burmese army had disappeared into the jungle after the surrender of the King. Without employment they carried on a guerrilla war against the British, roaming the country as dacoits or bandits. Eventually 32,000 troops were needed to control the countryside, and a heavily armed police force was required until the turn of the century.

76. Group of the 2nd Battalion Seaforth Highlanders, Black Mountain Expedition, 1888

The 2nd Battalion Seaforth Highlanders joined a punitive expedition on the North-West Frontier of India against the Asakis and Hassanzais, two tribes who had caused much trouble and murdered a Gurkha officer. The battalion was split into two columns which operated in the rough mountainous country for two months. After frequent skirmishes they succeeded in forcing the tribesmen to come to terms with the Indian government. Peace in this area of the frontier lasted until 1891.

77. *The 2nd Battalion Seaforth Highlanders on Diliari
Heights, Black Mountain Expedition, 1891*

*This regiment had been serving in India since 1871, and in
March 1891 returned once more to the North-West Frontier to
join the punitive expedition to Hazara in the Black Mountains.
They spent three months operating against the tribesmen until
law and order was, at last, restored. The regiment remained in
India and joined the Chitral relief force in 1895.*

78. 1st Battalion The King's Royal Rifle Corps, Chitral Campaign, 1895

This regiment are wearing Khaki uniforms, but with the
traditional black leather equipment associated with rifle
regiments in the British army. Here on the North-West
Frontier of India, they were fighting in one of the interminable
campaigns that the British army found itself in every few years.
Restless tribes, willing to fight their neighbours as well as the
British, and the overbearing might of Imperial Russia always in
the background left the area in constant turmoil.

79. *The fort at Chitral, Chitral Campaign, 1895*

The walls were 25 feet high with a tower at each corner. The fort was held by a small force of the 14th Sikh Regiment and the Kashmir Infantry. Under continual attack with a shortage of ammunition, the garrison was reduced to eating horseflesh. The Chitralis attempted to mine the fort, and through the gateway seen here, Lieutenant Harley led 40 of his Sikh Infantry on a sortie. They found the mineshaft, bayoneted the men inside and set a fuse to blow it up. The mineshaft exploded, killing more Chitralis, and the garrison was saved. Relief came after a 47 day siege.

80. *Kashmir Mountain Artillery in action, Chitral Campaign, 1895*

A small force was sent ahead of the main army to fight its way to relieve the Chitral Fort. This consisted of 400 men of the 32nd Punjab Pioneers, two mountain guns and a minimum of baggage. The men man-handled the guns over the mountains in deep snow with night temperatures below freezing. At Nisa Gol Valley they faced and fought 1,500 Chitralis; The mountain guns opened fire on the Chitralis and when this drove them into the open, the Infantry cut them down. The small force reached the fort and relieved the garrison 28 days after it had started out.

81. *Elephant field battery, Tirah campaign, 1897*

*At Peshawar a force of 35,000 men gathered together to deal
with the Afridi and Orakzai tribes on the Peshawar and Kohat
borders in the summer of 1897. Elephants were used to haul
the heavy 40-pounder guns over the mountain terrain in place
of 20 bullocks that would have been used on more level
country. The gunners are British, the drivers native Indians.*

82. *Gordon Highlanders storming Dargai Heights, 20th October, 1897*

A large number of tribesmen occupied the plateau and edge of the Dargai Heights. Few men were able to advance across the fire-swept zone. The colonel of the Gordon Highlanders addressed his men, 'The General says this hill must be taken at all costs, the Gordon Highlanders will take it'. The bugles rang, the pipes played and in 40 minutes the heights were captured. Thirty-three men of the regiment were killed or wounded.

83. *Artillery shelling the enemy, Sampaga Pass, Tirah
Campaign, 1897*

*On the 29th October the British force entered the pass, which
was approximately four miles long; the heights each side were
commanded by the enemy. The Artillery opened fire, and then
the Infantry attacked in force; after three hours fighting the
Afridi tribesmen retired.*

84. *G*eneral Sir William Lockhart and staff after the capture
of Sampaga Pass, Tirah Campaign, 1897

*The general and his staff are at ease on the rocks as the
wounded from the battle are carried by, on litters, to the base
hospital. The mules carrying the mountain artillery, baggage
and ammunition are also on the road. On the steep slope men
from the Gordon Highlanders can be seen resting after the
gruelling scramble over rough terrain.*

85. *Announcing terms to the Orakzai Maliks, Tirah campaign, 1897*

On 21st November the first advances towards peace were made by the Afridi tribesmen who sent their representatives to General Sir William Lockhart to investigate the terms he would offer them. It was not, however, until early the following year that peace terms were accepted and the campaign came to an end.

86. Cameron and Seaforth Highlanders bury their dead after the battle of Atbara, 1898

One brigade of General Kitchener's army had been sent up the Nile to Atbara, where the Nile divides into two. A Dervish army from Omdurman met them at the Atbara on 8th April 1898. The dervishes entrenched themselves behind a zariba. After an artillery bombardment the British advanced, halting to volley fire until they reached the zariba, which was honeycombed with rifle pits and trenches. The soldiers winkled them out until all the Dervishes were killed. The British army lost 80 killed and 479 wounded; the Dervishes lost 2,000, killed inside the zariba. In the photograph the dead Highlanders have been covered by greatcoats as the men dig their graves.

87. *The Emir Mahmud after the Battle of the Atbara, 8th April 1898*

The Khalifa's lieutenant, the Emir Mahmud, had been completely outmanoeuvred by the British, and with his back to the River Atbara was defeated by the Anglo-Egyptian army. Over 2,000 Dervishes were killed and Mahmud was captured. He is seen here with his captors, soldiers of the 10th Sudanese Regiment, one of six battalions that together had suffered 375 casualties in the fierce battle. The Emir was later sent back to Egypt.

88. *The Queen's Own Cameron Highlanders striking camps at Wad Hamed, 1898*

General Kitchener's army grouped at Wad Hamed, 58 miles from Omdurman to await reinforcements from Cairo. On 24th August 1898, the army moved off. They were the largest force ever to be seen in the Sudan, consisting of 8,200 British soldiers and 17,600 Egyptian and Sudanese. On 1st September, Lieutenant Winston Churchill with a patrol of the 21st Lancers noticed, 'a long black line moving forward, four miles from end to end and in five great divisions, perhaps 40,000 hostile spear-points spread a sparkling cloud.' It was the Khalifa's host coming to battle.

89. *General Kitchener directing the Battle of Omdurman, 2nd September, 1898*

At the age of 42, Kitchener was appointed Commander-in-Chief of the Egyptian army with the rank of Major General. He became Commander-in-Chief of the Anglo-Egyptian army in 1898. His newly trained Egyptian forces, together with the British army, defeated the Khalifa, culminating in the battle of Omdurman where the Dervish power in the Sudan was broken and General Gordon's murder was avenged.

90. *View over the heads of the Grenadier Guards with the Dervishes advancing, Omdurman, 2nd September 1898*

In front of the guards is a thornbush zariba to impede the enemy. They succeeded in getting to within 800 yards and opened a rapid and heavy rifle fire. Among those who fell were Charles Williams from The Daily Chronicle, *who died with a bullet through the head and Colonel Rhodes, from* The Times, *who was shot through the shoulder.*

91. *The Royal Warwickshire Regiment resting after the Battle of Omdurman*

The first battalion had been part of the garrison in Egypt and had hurried south to join General Kitchener's army. They had fought in the Battle of the Atbara, and came into action at Omdurman soon after the Grenadier Guards opened fire on the Dervishes. The Infantry set their sights at 2,000 yards, while the Artillery batteries had opened fire five minutes before at a range of 2,700 yards, the shells bursting right in the enemy's ranks, causing havoc, death and destruction.

92. Dervishes lying dead on the battlefield, Omdurman, 1898

For five hours the Dervishes launched spirited and brave
attacks against the British army, but all was destroyed by the
accurate and steady fire of disciplined British troops. After the
battle the Egyptian and Sudanese soldiers picked over the
bodies for any available loot.

93. The Royal Munster Fusiliers, South Africa, 1899

These soldiers are drawn up in a typical defensive position used since the days of Napoleon. In the colonial wars it had served well against undisciplined hordes, unused to the steady fire of the trained soldier. This time the British were in conflict with a foe well-armed with rifles and with some tactical competence.

94. *Mounted Rifles packing up at Modder River, South Africa, 1900*

As the Boers were mainly a mounted force, a greater mobility was required by the British, who formed mounted Infantry regiments. These men carried rifles instead of the short-range Cavalry carbine and fought on foot using the horse to carry them to the combat area. Machine guns were mounted on wheels and drawn by the horses, to be used in the same manner.

95. *British troops on the defence at Naauwpoort, November 1899*

Naauwpoort was a strategic railway junction and was evacuated by the British on 1st November 1899. It was, however, retaken on 19th November. The soldiers are preparing to fire in volleys. The middle rank is ready to fire; as soon as they have done so they step back to reload, the kneeling line stands up to take their place and rear line moves forward to the kneeling position.

96. *Mounted rifles at De Aar, January, 1900*

*Rapid movement over the veld required Cavalry, which the
British were very short of. Field Marshal Lord Roberts made
strenuous efforts to build up a mounted Infantry. Regiments of
the line were instructed to raise a company of mounted men
from soldiers who could ride. The town of De Aar was a
railway junction between the Cape and the Transvaal.*

**97. *The Cape Garrison Artillery firing across the Modder
River, January 1900***

*It was very hot at this time of the year and 21 men died from
sunstroke, many of whom were reservists who had come up
from the Cape – such as these artillerymen. The guns are 12-
pounders, breech-loading with hydraulic carriage; they fired a
lyddite shell with a 50-yard killing range.*

98. *A casualty for the field hospital being loaded into an*
ambulance, Modder River, January, 1900

The Royal Army Medical Corps were a very efficent body of
men during the Boer War. Of the 22,000 casualties in the war,
most survived. Every soldier carried a field dressing and in the
dry, hot veld, wounds tended to dry and heal without
infection. High velocity bullets tended to go straight through
the body; the hard-cased bullet would leave only a bruise at its
entry.

99. *The Worcestershire Regiment defending New Zealand Hill, Slingerfontein, 1900*

The regiment lost 15 men killed and 29 wounded before they were driven back to Slingersfontein, the men had flaps to their pith helmets to offer some protection against the fierce African sun. They were armed with the Lee Enfield Mark I Rifle, introduced in 1895, and sighted for up to 3,500 yards.

100. Roll-call after Dordrecht, 15th February, 1900

General Brabant delivered a night assault on the Boer
entrenchments and a day later Dordrecht fell to the British.
From there the Orange Free State was invaded. In the
background a sergeant is calling a roll-call of the dead and
wounded. In the foreground the wounded are tended before
being taken to the hospital.

101. *Gordon Highlander signallers at Euslin, South Africa, 1900*

Signalling with a heliograph was the common form of communication during the war in South Africa. This was a controlled mirror on a tripod, flashing the sun's reflection in Morse code. It could be read at a range of 30 miles or more, but, of course, relied on the weather. Every regiment had its own heliograph section, but telegraphic and balloon signalling was in the hands of the Royal Engineers.

102. Ammunition Column, 1900

One of Field Marshal Lord Roberts' ammunition columns en
route to Kimberly in February, 1900. The town was relieved on
15th February by General French, having been under siege
since 14th October 1899. As well as being a diamond centre, it
was served by the railway that ran from the Cape to Rhodesia.

103. *The Warwickshire Regiment skirmishing with the Boers,*
April 1900

This was at Weppener, east of Bloemfontein. The British had a
force of 1,600 men at Weppener, and were besieged by the
Boers until relieved on 24th April, 1900. On 13th March Lord
Roberts entered Bloemfontein, but the war did not end with
the capture of the main Boer cities. The British held the towns
but not the open veld.

104. Rest halt, the Guard's Brigade, May, 1900

These battle-hardened guardsmen look the veterans they were.
Their khaki uniform was of a light colour, a little faded here.
The Slade Wallace equipment was not pipe-clayed, and their
buttons were left dull; Boer marksmanship made it necessary
to be inconspicuous. Officers removed their badges of rank but
wore a patch on the back of their helmets so that they would
be recognized by their men.

105. Australian Mounted Rifles, South Africa, 1900

*The British received considerable support from the Empire,
and in particular Canada, Australia and New Zealand.
Australia had 28,000 men in the field by the end of the war.
Most of them as mounted rifles. Although they fought well,
discipline was slack and officers were unable to keep control.
On one occasion, as they sat around the fireside in camp
without a guard, they were attacked; 20 were shot dead and 40
wounded, most of the others surrendered and a large and
valuable convoy of ammunition fell into the Boers' hands. In
battle their reputation was better. At Brakfontein in August
1900, 500 Australians fought off 3,000 Boers for 11 days before
relief came. Six Australians were awarded the Victoria Cross
during the war.*

106. 'Betsey', the field gun, Peking, 1900

The foreign legations in the city were under siege for 55 days during the Boxer Rebellion, and to protect the ambassadors and ministers there was a mixed force of troops from the various legations. The only field gun within the legation compound was 'Our Betsey', or 'The International'. It was an old British gun barrel discovered in a Chinese junk shop, mounted on an Italian gun carriage, that fired Russian ammunition, and was manned by the British Royal Marine Light Infantry!

107. **Unloading the baggage of the Bombay Cavalry, Siege of Peking, *1900***

The relief force to rescue the legations in Peking composed around 16,000 men. The only cavalry that was of any use was that from the Indian army; the Japanese had only the cavalry regiment, so poor in quality that only 60 horses out of 400 reached Peking! The 6th United States Cavalry landed at Taku but their horses were still unfit after the voyage; apart from a few Cossacks, all the cavalry work was carried out by the Indian troops.

108. Ruins of the legations at Peking, 1900

The area controlled by the Allies during the siege comprised the British, United States, German, Russian, Japanese and Spanish legations. Most of the French legation was overrun by August, while the Austrian, Italian and Dutch legations – which were outside the perimeter – were destroyed by fire. The legation quarter was in the Tatar City, adjacent to the Forbidden City.

109. Execution of Boxers with the Allies looking on, Peking, 1900

On 14th August at 3.00 pm. British-Indian regiments entered Peking by crawling under the water gate at the Tatar City Wall, and the central gates were flung open to receive the rescuing British troops. The siege was over after 55 days. Over 200 people had been killed and wounded in the legation; in the country itself 30,000 Christian Chinese were killed by the Boxers. Two weeks after the siege a victory parade was held marching through the city. Later some of the Boxers who had been captured were beheaded in public, watched by the Allied soldiers.

***110. Sikh Infantry on the steps of the Ch,I Nien Temple,
Peking, 1900***

*The Ch,I Nien, hall of annual prayers was at the Temple of
Heaven, where the Chinese Emperor would pray for a good
harvest. After the siege the men of the regiment posed here
with their British officers. Peace negotiations got slowly under
way and were signed on 7th September 1901, over a year after
the legations had been relieved. Ten days later the last of the
international troops left Peking.*

III. British officers talking to Tibetan Lamas, Tibet, 1903

*Once again fear of Russian influence in Asia caused the British
government to send Colonel Francis Edward Younghusband
with an army of 3,000 men into Tibet. Three engagements
were fought before negotiations took place. Tibetan Lamas are
seen here acting as envoys from the Dalai Lama, speaking to
British officers.*

112. The British camp at Phari Jong, Tibet, 1904

*By June 1904 the Dalai Lama had made no attempt to
negotiate with the British force, who moved forward on to
Lhasa. Another small action was fought here and the British
entered the city in August, where treaty was successfully agreed
upon at last.*

113. *Assembly of tribal leaders to hear the British terms,*
Bazar Valley, 1908

Major General Wilcocks at Walai seated at the table and
signing the peace treaty. The rifles deposited by the tribesmen
as a security are on the ground in front of them.

ACKNOWLEDGEMENTS

The author and publisher would like to thank the following for permission to reproduce photographs:

Hawkes Bay Art Gallery and Museum: 40–44; Imperial War Museum: 24, 25, 28, 32, 34, 35; India Office Library: 22, 23, 26, 52, 53, 59, 73–75, 81; National Army Museum: 1–10, 19, 20, 27, 29-31, 33, 36, 38, 39, 45–51, 54–58, 60–67, 76–80, 83–88, 106–113; Queen's Own Highlanders Regimental Museum: 68; Royal Commonwealth Society: 69–72; Science Museum: 11, 13–18, 21; Victoria and Albert Museum: 12; Author's Collection: 82, 89–105.